Simply Amazed

By
Brenda Wilson Billings

Copyright © 2021 Brenda Wilson Billings

No part of this book may be reproduced or transmitted in any form or by any means: graphic, electronic, or mechanical, including photocopying, recording, taping, or by any information storage retrieval system without permission, in writing, of the publisher or author.

Lowbar Publishing Company
905 S. Douglas Ave.
Nashville, Tennessee 37204
615-972-2842
Lowbarpublishingcompany@gmail.com www.Lowbarbookstore.com
Author: Brenda Wilson Billings
Editor: Terrica W.
Pictures: Calvin C. Barlow, Jr.
Format Artist: Alisha A.
Graphic and Cover Design Artist: Sharon B.

Printed in the United States of America
ISBN: 978-1-7329202-7-9
For additional information or to contact the author for workshops or seminars, please email the author, or Lowbar Publishing Company.

Table of Contents

Foreword vii

Poem of Dedication viii

Simply Amazed viii

Recognition ix

Poems about Pastors 1

    Reverend Kareem A. Crump 2

    Pastor's Anniversary 3

    A Pastor 4

    Reverend Barlow 5

Poems about Fathers 7

    A Father 8

    A Father's Love 9

Poems about Music 11

    A Song 12

    Adult Choir Day 13

Poems about Mothers 15

    A Woman Of God 16

    A Mother 17

A Praying Mother 18

Dear Mother 19

I Love You Mother 20

Women Walking In Our Season 21

Poems About The Savior 23

Lord, Just Let Me Walk With You 24

He Hears My Prayer 25

My God 26

So Many Times 27

God Blesses All Of His Children 28

God Has Given Love 29

Lord Of My Life 30

God Takes Care 31

I Always Call On You Lord 32

God Is My Joy Each Day 33

Lord, What A Wonderful Day 34

There Is No One Like The Lord 35

If It Hadn't Been For You 36

God Is Creator 37

We Were Made In His Image 38

Savior 39

Poems of Comfort 41

The Pain Of A Shed Tear 42

When You're In Despair 43

When You See Something Bad 44

Every Bridge 45

When I Was Down...46

When I'm In Trouble...47

Jesus, Sweet Jesus..48

Jesus 49

Just When I Need Him Most 50

When Jesus Came..51

If You Have A Dream..52

Poems of Hope..53

Today 54

What A Blessing 55

Miscellaneous Poems 57

What Can I Teach? 58

I Am So Wondrously Blessed...59

Be Thankful..60

On Stormy Nights..61

When A LOVED One Is Gone..62

Restoring Good Health 63

Just To Keep Your Commandments 64

A Testimony...65

Even In My Sin..66

With All My Heart...67

An Ode to a Friend **69**
    Sister Wilma Mcgee...70
Remembering Mama..**71**
    Little Girl Sucking Her Thumb...79
    Miss You 80

Foreword

My Brothers and Sisters ~

We are blessed to have our Sister, Brenda Wilson Billings, inspirational writings. Brenda gives us resources for our Spiritual Journey in time of prayer and meditation. In reading *Simply Amazed*, you will have inner peace, understanding, wholeness, strength, love, grace, wisdom, and power. My faith and patience have increased. My mind is refocused on Him. We must help one another and remember all things are possible to Him who believes.

Simply Amazed

Deacon Stanley B. Young

POEM OF DEDICATION

Simply Amazed

I'm simply amazed at all the wonderful things that God has done.

I'm simply amazed at all the victories and battles that we have won.

When I think of how He brought me out,

It simply amazes me to see all the miracles He has brought about.

The Lord is my light. He brightens every day;

He's a healer, a deliverer. Throughout it all, He'll make a way.

So, no matter where you come from or how you were raised.

He has an answer to every problem,

And I'm simply amazed.

Brenda Wilson Billings

Recognition

Reverend Earnest O. King

Ms. Mildred Gregory

Ms. Leteacha Carr

A special thanks goes out to

Reverend Andy A. Carr

Who named the book,

Simply Amazed

Pastor Kareem & First Lady LaTonya Crump

While we take the time to reflect on what we call *"Special Days"*, I believe these days are set in divine order. It allows us to exercise biblical principles such as honor and love. These days are times we remember, the good times when Mother showed her unconditional love or our Father took the time to show us life lessons in his own unique way, even honoring and loving on those who served to protect our country. So, we must cherish *special days*, and that will cause *special moments*, which bring about *special memories*. In conclusion, let us celebrate one another where we will discover what matters most – love.

Signed in Love,
Dr. Kareem A. Crump, B.R.E., D.D.

Poems about Pastors

Jeremiah 3:15

And I will give you pastors according to mine heart, which shall feed you with knowledge and understanding.

Reverend Kareem A. Crump

Reverend Crump is a great Preacher.
In so many ways,
He gently leads and guides us
And gives us words of praise.

I haven't known him a long time,
But, yet, and still,
He teaches us about the Bible
And doing God's will.

So, continue to be a blessing
To us at Morning View;
We appreciate you and love you
For all that you do.

Pastor's Anniversary

There are so many things
That we could give,
But one thing we want to give you
Are your flowers, while you live!

Words cannot express all the love
We have inside,
But as we mature in Jesus,
He'll be our heavenly guide.

So, as this Anniversary closes,
Until another precious day,
Let Jesus guide you and keep you
In His own special way.

A Pastor

A Pastor is a leader.
He works both night and day.
And, if we have a problem,
He will steer us in the right way.

A Pastor is an example.
We learn from how he lives.
He is unique because God leads him
By the power that He gives.

A Pastor is not only special,
But he is a man of God.
He is called by the Almighty on high
To preach against all odds.

Let us respect and give him reverence,
And our undivided love
For a Pastor represents Jesus.
He is our gift from God above.

Reverend Barlow

Reverend Barlow will help you in any way that he can.

He is a man of GOD and a family man.

He has to be knowledgeable,

For reading is a part of his job.

He preaches and teaches from the word of GOD.

He should be honored and respected everywhere.

For in his ministry, he will show you that he cares.

Just knowing him has been a delight.

He preaches the truth and will tell you what is right.

If words could be something that I could give,

I want to give him his flowers while he lives.

So, GOD bless you, Reverend Barlow,

Your wife and family too.

Keep up the good work, and GOD will see you through.

Poems about Fathers

Colossians 3:21

*Fathers, provoke not your children to anger,
lest they be discouraged.*

A Father

A Father is such a special one,
Someone to always hold dear to your heart.
Whether for a daughter or a son,
A Father plays an important part.

A Father doesn't have an easy job,
Providing and loving all his children and their mother.
Of all the presents in the world,
A Father's love is like none other.

And, if you don't have a Father in your life,
But you have an uncle, brother, or father image,
Then, you are still blessed,
Because the love of this male companion
Is love, and love at its best.

So, my prayer for all the Fathers
On this Father's Day
Is to have that bond to keep your families together,
And to always have joy, love, peace,
And a blessed life forever.

HAPPY FATHER'S DAY

A Father's Love

There is nothing like a Father's love,
A love that is blessed from up above.
A Father figure is a blessing too,
And our Heavenly Father will see us through.

The Father is the head of his home.
And each of his children, a Father will own.
A brother or uncle or a Grandpa too,
Can be a Father and a mentor for you.

So, as we celebrate Fathers on this Father's Day,
Whether your Father is with you or whether he is gone,
Let us remember our Heavenly Father above
And know we are never left alone.

May Father's Day bring you joy and happiness.
And, by honoring your father and mother,
You will be blessed.

HAPPY FATHER'S DAY

Poems about Music

Psalm 150:1

Praise ye the L<small>ORD</small>. *Praise God in his sanctuary: praise him in the firmament of his power.*

A Song

A song is a way of giving praise to God,
A way of rendering service to Jesus our Lord.
As our voices blend in one by one,
We praise His name on one accord.

Whether we sing the high notes or the low notes in the bass,
The unity of the choir makes it a special place.
The Bible says, "I love the Lord because He hath heard
My voice and my supplications."
So, as we lift our voices to sing His praises,
Let us remember God can heal any situation.

So, on this Annual Choir Day, may we sing and praise Him,
Knowing that Jesus is the way.

Adult Choir Day

God starts off each day with a song.
The little birdies sing His praises all day long.
In the summer, you can hear the children playing with glee,
And that is how I think heaven will be.

In celebrating our Adult Choir's Annual Day,
It is a chance for us to sing and a chance to pray.
As our choir sings from their hearts within,
It is a time to see miracles,
And a time to begin.

You will not go away with an empty cup.
Your heart and soul will be lifted and filled up.
So, sing on choir, and give God the praise.
Honor Him always, for the rest of your days.

Psalms 98 says:
"O sing unto the Lord a new song."
And, as we unite one to another,
Let us love and respect
Our Sisters and Brothers.
On this special Annual Day,
Let us love and be led in God's own special way.

HAPPY ADULT CHOIR'S ANNUAL DAY

Poems about Mothers

Proverbs 31:10

Who can find a virtuous woman? For her price is far above rubies

A Woman Of God

She carries herself in a special way;
And never does she cease to pray.
In God, she trusts to make a way;
She lives for God. He won't let her stray.

She is the apple's eye to a certain man,
And does for him whatever she can.
Today, women have a special place.
She lives in the word and grows in grace.
We must raise and encourage our own.
A woman will nurture and teach children until they're grown.

So, on this day let us be on one accord
And be the woman God is looking for.
May Woman's Day be a blessing from God above,
And may we, as women, dwell together in love.

A Mother

There's a song that says,
"A Mother loves her children all of the time"
But, if she really is a mother,
She's going to love your children and also mine.

A Mother is a leader.
She teaches her children right.
Her never dying love
Will guide them to the light.

A Mother is a vessel
Used to travel here from up above,
And each child she carries
Is a symbol of God's love.

So, on this Mother's Day,
May we love all the little ones,
As well as the grownups too,
And thank God above
For the way that He's brought us through.

And let us not forget the fathers too on this great day.
Just always respect and love your Mom and Dad,
And God will make a way.

A Praying Mother

You worried about me

When I was going wrong,

But your faith in God

Helped keep you strong.

You prayed for me.

You shed some tears,

But through it all,

You persevered.

And now, I know you

Didn't give up on me.

I thank and praise God

For His light to see.

The never wavering trust you had

Has given me hope and

Made me glad.

For God has answered

Your prayers for me,

And I'm glad to be all that I can be.

Dear Mother

Thank you for your kindness
And help bringing me to earth,
For guiding me to Christ
And giving me self-worth.
Your love means so much.
I could never say enough.
My life, you have touched,
Even when times did get rough.

So may you live long
And may you have peace.
May you prosper daily
And your life never cease.
For God, I feel, has made you
According to His will.
You've done a great job.
Your shoes only you can fill.

And maybe you feel down sometimes,
Or even get depressed,
But smile on anyway.
For Mom, you are the best.

I Love You Mother

I love you so dear, Mother.
You mean so much to me.
Your teachings and your loving
Have shaped me into me.

I could never say thank you enough
For all you've done for me,
Your beauty and your virtue
For all the world to see.

And though you are not famous,
You mean so very much.
My love for you is never dying,
For my life you've blessed and touched.

Women Walking In Our Season

As women, we are growing by grace,
And each of us has a special place.
We are mothers, teachers, and we're all well blessed.
Some are doctors, lawyers. In all, do we find success.

No matter the season you're walking in,
We must all focus on Christ,
Our savior and our friend.

A woman plays an important role,
Knowing Christ is Lord and is in control.
Let us celebrate life and Women's Day,
For God is still making a way.

May Woman's Day be a blessing to all of you.
It is a great day for Morning View.

Poems About The Savior

Luke 1:47

And my spirit hath rejoiced in God my Saviour.

Lord, Just Let Me Walk With You

Lord, just let me walk with you.

Hold my hand and keep me nearby.

In all the earth, there is none like you.

Conquer everything, I fear.

Let my life be filled with joy.

Lighten my every burden too.

You are my everlasting,

God.

I believe you'll see me through.

He Hears My Prayer

The Lord, He hears my prayer
And answers my every need.
He gives His tender care
And blesses my life indeed.

He's the answer
Of my every need.
He inspires me to succeed.
He knows my every desire
And lifts my spirits higher.

My God

My God, He lifted me when I was burdened down.

He set my soul free and turned my life around.

So, if you are burdened and want someone to care.

Call on Lord Jesus, for He is everywhere.

So Many Times

So many times, when I wasn't thinking,
God stepped in; He thought for me.
So many times, He came to my rescue.
I believe He is one in three.

He protected me from all harm and danger.
He was not a stranger.
He never put me away in anger.
He was my Creator born in a manger.

On Calvary, He was pierced in the side,
Hung His head, and then He died.
Rose on Sunday from being crucified,
He has become my Heavenly guide.

I give Him constant praise.
He has blessed all my days.
Out of nowhere, He has made a way.
I thank Him for His Amazing Grace.

God Blesses All Of His Children

God blesses all His children.
Young or old, He will make a way,
Though some are homeless and some are ill,
He blesses each in His will.

God blesses all His children.
Some are dying yet and still,
He promises everlasting life.
He blesses each in His will.

God Has Given Love

God has given love through many generations.

He has given love through tons of situations.

To the confused,

He has straightened up minds.

To the sick,

He has healed all kinds.

To the lonely, He has been a friend.

To the faithful,

He has endured to the end.

Lord Of My Life

Lord of my life, I come to thee,
Wounded in spirit and soul.
Give me the will to live and be free.
Oh, forever our love will be.

Down kneeling in this flesh, I pray.
Keep and watch over me.
Prepare me for thy will each day
And always take care of me.

God Takes Care

God takes good care of His own,
Whether we are weak or strong.
His watching daily over us
Gives us the will to go on.

God takes good care of His own.
Yes, He knows every care that we own.
His love and grace
Prepare us a place
So, we can live and not do wrong.

I Always Call On You Lord

I always call on you, Lord,

To make a way for me.

You never fail to answer

Even the smallest plea.

Without you, I could not make it,

And with you, I will not fall.

You have blessed my days, Lord.

You are my all in all.

God Is My Joy Each Day

God is my joy each day.

He hears me each time I pray.

Though sometimes up

And sometimes down,

The world can't take my joy away.

There are days when loved ones leave.

This cold and cruel world sometimes gets to me,

But every day to Him I bow.

I know His friendship is comforting.

Savior of mine,

My joy each day,

Help me to follow

And not to stray.

There are times when I feel low,

But You help me along the road.

Lord, What A Wonderful Day

Lord, what a wonderful day
You have brought.
A moment captured,
A blessed thought,
Your mighty hands
Have blessed our lives.
A miracle,
A sweet surprise,
A gentle touch
Precious as gold,
A story in each of us is told.
For in the hearts of young and old,
Our lives have begun to unfold.

There Is No One Like The Lord

There is no one and nothing like the Lord.
His power to heal and bless
Has given me so much happiness.
The Lord works in mysterious ways.
He can LOVE, HEAL, and BLESS all your days.

There is no one and nothing like the Lord.
There is nothing that He cannot do.
He blesses all of us throughout our lives.
He can work out things that do not seem real.
He performs miracles, and He can heal.

The Lord is great and worthy to be praised.
Trust Him to bless all your days.

If It Hadn't Been For You

Lord, if it had not been for you,
I could not do all that I do.
If you had not looked out for me,
I could not live my lifetime through.
For when despair enters in,
I find a new way to begin, and
All the joy and strength from you
Let me know that I can win.

So, I sing a song of praise, and I thank you in every way.
You have blessed me so wondrously.
Thanks for letting me be me.

God Is Creator

GOD is creator, creator of all,
From mountain high to valley small.
He made man from the dust of the ground.
None greater than Him has ever been found.

In GOD's CREATION, He made man and woman.
He did not stop there; He also made the child and
A glorious world to place them in.
God made the earth in His own divine style.

GOD is creator, creator of all.
His power never fails.
In His dominion, there is nothing He can't do.
Try Him today. He will see you through.

We Were Made In His Image

We were made in His image,
A creation of His own.
We were drawn from the dust,
And He gave us a song.
To love all His children,
To do right instead of wrong,
We are children of the Most High.
So, let us try to get along.

Savior

My heart belongs to you.
Daily, I pray, and I thank-you for seeing me through.

Precious life each day from you to me,
I once was sightless, but now I see.

Holy Redeemer, shine your light on me.
Enable me to be whole and free.
You hold in your hands that golden key
To unlock and deliver me.

Poems of Comfort

John 14:16

*And I will pray the Father, and he shall give you another **Comforter**, that he may abide with you forever.*

The Pain Of A Shed Tear

The pain of a shed tear,
It releases all the pain.
Shedding a tear
Releases all pain,
But know that God is nearby.
It's not always going to rain.

The enemy is always there,
But God is the one in charge.
So, as we go through pain,
He'll heal us wherever we are.

When You're In Despair

When you are in despair and
Cannot see your way,
Call on the name of Jesus
To brighten your day.

When you have a problem
That you cannot seem to solve,
Remember, there is nothing too big
Or too hard for GOD.

So, try Him when you are down.
When you cannot see your way,
Receive that blessing from the Lord today.

When You See Something Bad

When you see something bad happen,
In any circumstance,
Try to look for the good.
We're not here just by chance.

For GOD made everything, and
All He made is good.
Even things like death can somehow be understood.

The Lord made us from the dust of the earth, and
The life that he gave
Is worth more than anything else.
So, I praise Him now, and when I'm gone,
I hope to be with Him and make heaven my home.

Every Bridge

Every bridge
I try to build,
The devil tears it down.
But, in spite of it all,
My God still allows me to go across,
Just like the children of Israel
Who got through anyway!
So, I just keep building bridges
Each and every day.

God is going to make a way
As sure as I kneel to pray
He will step in and brighten
Each, and every day.

When I Was Down

When I was down and out,
Away from friends and loved ones,
When no one seemed to care,
My Jesus was there.
And while troubles were near
And I could not see my way,
He was planning my victory
For a brighter day.

So, through all the sorrow
And all the pain,
Learn to appreciate the sun and the rain.
For He will lift you up
And will give you a song.
He will forgive you for everything
You have done wrong.

Every day, I thank Him
For seeing me through,
And I recognize Him
In all that I do.

When I'm In Trouble

When I am in trouble,

Lord, deliver me.

When I am burdened,

Lord, set me free

When I have done wrong

Or cannot see,

Mercy is my song,

And healing is my plea.

Jesus, Sweet Jesus

Jesus, sweet Jesus,

Come inside of me.

Jesus, sweet Jesus,

Help my eyes to see.

In the midst of trials,

In the midst of failure,

Be my sweet friend,

Jesus.

Jesus

Jesus, Jesus,
The Master is He.
Let us glorify Him,
One and Three.

Heavenly angels
Rejoice at His name.
Since He came to earth,
Nothing has been the same.

Jesus, Jesus,
How sweet the sound.
Glory and honor
To Him abound.

Just When I Need Him Most

Just when I need Him most,
He will be there.
Just when I think I will falter,
He will answer my prayer.

The Lord is my Savior.
In Him, I will abide.
He has time to listen
To each and every cry.

Just when I think it is over,
He will protect me.
Jesus gave it all
With his blood on Calvary.

When Jesus Came

When Jesus came,
The world was blessed.

And, in His name,
You will find happiness.
For happiness is in knowing the Lord,
And sin and shame,
We cannot afford.

Lift His name!
Oh, lift His name!

Do not look back.
Be glad He came.
He has power to save your soul.
Put your trust in Him,
For He is in control.

If You Have A Dream

If you have a dream,

If you have a goal at hand,

You will need the Lord

To help you make a stand.

If you have hope,

If you do not fear,

He will help you cope,

And your dream will become real.

Poems of Hope

Psalm 38:15

For in thee, O Lord, *do I* **hope**: *thou wilt hear,*
O Lord my God.

Today

Today is a new day,
A brand-new start to make,
Following Lord Jesus,
Each footstep He takes.
The past is behind me.
The future is before me.
I am doing what needs to be done
So tomorrow will be grand.

What A Blessing

What a blessing to wake up each morning.
What a blessing to wake up each day.
You may not think you are getting a blessing,
But it's a blessing to wake up each day.
You may be torn,
And you may be blue.
But it is a blessing to wake up each day,
For I know God will see you through.

Miscellaneous Poems

John 14:26

*But the Comforter, which is the Holy Ghost, whom the Father will send in my name, he shall **teach** you all things, and bring all things to your remembrance, whatsoever I have said unto you.*

Simply Amazed

What Can I Teach?

You can teach a little child.
You can make a difference.
You make him or her smile?

Jesus always loved children
In His life here on Earth,
Teaching and preaching to give them some self-worth.

Can I dry a tear
When am I crying myself?
How can I hold up
When I do not know what
To do?

God gives us strength,
Enough for us to bear.
So, pray as you raise your children,
If they are with you or elsewhere.

I Am So Wondrously Blessed

I am so wondrously blessed.
God has truly been there for me.
His love for me has passed the test.
Daily, He moves and keeps me free.

Sometimes, I am up
And sometimes down,
But through it all,
He stays around.

Never has He given up on me.
He cleaned me up
And blessed me to see
I am so wondrously blessed.

He has turned my enemies away.
He has kept me in His arms, oh yes,
And turned my midnights into day.

Be Thankful

Be thankful for everything you have
And give God all the praise,
For we don't deserve a thing,
But He blesses us any way.

Whether a job, a car, or even a home,
Whether good health and strength, or just a room,
God blesses all of us at His best.
For when we wake up, we find that we are blessed.

On Stormy Nights

On stormy nights,
When you are all alone,
It is so nice to linger
At His throne.

He shelters His own
With tender care.
Through thunder and lightning,
He will be right there.

On sunny days,
When the world seems so sweet,
Jesus will make your whole life complete.

Whether it is sunny or rainy,
Jesus will sooth and bring peace about.

Call Him each day.
He will make all your dark days bright again.
Jesus has love far above all men.
Open your room for His love to come in.

When A LOVED One Is Gone

I know it is hard
When a loved one is gone,

But memory is a blessing.
So, we can carry on.

Sometimes, we think of something
Funny they said,
And we hold on to that moment
Without sadness instead.

God is all powerful,
And He will give us grace.
He can heal and comfort
Each tearful face.

Praise Him always
And don't give in.
His will be done,
As He lets us re-begin.

Restoring Good Health

Lord, there are so many
Things that I must do,
But I know if I take one step,
Then you will take two.
Healing takes time, just
Like anything else,
And I know, in Your own time.
I will be blessed to restore good health.

If I climb my mountain daily,
I will soon reach the top.
And, as I count all my blessings,
There will be no reason to stop.
For I know you are there with me,
All the way through.
So daily, Lord, guide me to do what is pleasing to you.

Just To Keep Your Commandments

When I was young,

I knew about Jesus,

And, as the world,

I was doing my thing.

But now I long

Just to keep His commandments

And praise His name when I sing.

Oh, Heavenly Father

Here I am

Just to say

How glad I am,

To be Your child

And praise Your name,

Just to keep Your commandments

Is what I aim.

A Testimony

If you have gone through something,
You have a testimony.
Though storms come in our lives,
We can depend on God and Him alone.
Though winds may blow
And loved ones leave,
You have a testimony,
If you just believe.

So, let us give praise to God
And share what He has done.
And let our testimony be
About the great race that we have won.

Even In My Sin

He looks out for me.
One day, he came in and set my soul free,
Gave me peace of mind,
And opened my heart.
He left the past behind
And took a brand-new start.

Jesus is my King
And special to me too,
Died on Calvary
And carried me through.
Oh, what a joy to me He has shared!
Let us praise Him to the highest
Everywhere!

With All My Heart

With all my heart and soul,
I trust in Jesus Christ.
He keeps and takes control
Of everything in my life.

And when I am burdened down,
He eases all my pain.
And daily, as I travel,
I can be whole again.

An Ode to a Friend

John 15:13

*Greater love hath no man than this, that a man lay down his life for his **friends**.*

Sister Wilma McGee

John 15:13

*Greater love hath no man than this, that a man lay down his life for his **friends**.*

When I met Sister McGee,
I could see her glow.
Like a haloed angel,
Her radiance is felt anywhere she goes.

She is a lady of grace,
Nice as she can be,
And her love for God
Is what I first could see.

Sister McGee has always
Been nice and kind.
So, I could not exclude her
Because she stays on my mind.

So, keep writing, Sister McGee,
And doing what you do.
I will always love you!

Remembering Mama

Proverbs 23:22

*Hearken unto thy father that begat thee, and despise not thy **mother** when she is old.*

Mama,

>Do you remember the time when I was in the hospital, and you came to see me? You walked in the door with your grace and gray hair, and the patients gathered around you. They said, "Got any candy, gum, cigarettes, or a nickel?" You said you didn't have enough sense to be afraid of them, and you came to see me every day.

Do You Remember?

Once when I was gone astray,
Even while I was put away,
You loved me with your special prayer,
I made it out because you were there.

Do You Remember?

Mama,

Do you remember when I was 13 and I wanted a bra? You took me to the department store. The lady measured me and said, "Oh, we don't have any that small." And I started crying in the store. Then, later, you bought me one any way.

Do You Remember?

Even though I was rather small,
You loved me and helped me stand up tall.
You were always nice to me.
You gave me hope and victory.

Do You Remember?

Mama,

Remember when I was 15 and was trying to eat a potato chip? I started hyperventilating, and I could not breathe? And you picked me up and took me outside where I could get some air?

Do You Remember?

You were strong.
You were tall.
You were definitely
My all and all.

Do You Remember?

Mama,

    Remember when we were walking to church, and a car backed up on me and hit me below my heart? And you let the man driving take us to the hospital?

    Do You Remember?

    Sometimes, you could not help
    Whatever would be,
    But you always, always,
    Looked out for me.

    Do You Remember?

Mama,

    Remember when you sent me to take my little brother to a birthday party so he would not fall on the ice? But I fell on the ice instead?

    Do You Remember?

    You trusted me to give him care,
    But we made it through,
    Through God, in prayer.

    Do You Remember?

Mama,

>Remember when I was 3 years old, and we walked my older brother to school? I would cry all the way home, because I was too young to go.

Do You Remember?

I wanted to go to school so bad,
But I was not old enough.
The trip back and forth
Was really, really, rough.

Do You Remember?

Mama,

>Remember when I was 9 months pregnant? I said, "I don't know if I want to have a baby." You told me I should have thought about that before then.

Do You Remember?

The baby was a blessing.
For when you and Dad got old,
He took the best care of you both
And put his life on hold.

Do You Remember?

Mama,

> Remember the time we went to my youngest brother's PH.D. ceremony? Then, we went to dinner with all the family. After that, we all went our separate ways. You said, "We had a good time."

> Do You Remember?

> We were all having a really good time.
> That memory often stays on my mind.

> Do You Remember?

Mama,

> Remember when you were frying something on the stove and went out of the kitchen to talk on the phone, then the skillet caught on fire? You came in the kitchen and took the skillet and put it in the oven, and the fire went out. But the walls were all sooty, and we had to wash the walls before Daddy got home from work that night.

> Do You Remember?

> You were smart
> In so many ways,
> And I'll always
> Remember those kinds of days.

> Do You Remember?

Mama,

When I last saw you, you were ill. You suffered two weeks. When you began to cry out because of your pain, I held your hand and told you it would be o.k.

And then, you passed away. There were flowers everywhere at your funeral. Right before they closed your casket, I went to you, touched your arm, and the last words I said to you were, "Goodbye Mama, you'll be alright." And I believe you are alright. You may have been looking down from Heaven when I touched you.

> God does not reveal everything to us.
> But I know if you are in His Hands,
> You are really alright.
> Always Remember That, Mama.

Yes, I remember so many things about Mama. It does not make me sad to think of her. Instead, it makes me happy. I lost her in 2020, but I'll always remember the wonderful woman she was. If I could have half of what she had to offer, I would be proud of myself.

She was charming, graceful, full of life and love. She loved children and loved all of us. She would always say, "Teach the babies."

Sometimes, I don't know the full extent of my calling, but, if I could be like my mother, that would be my highest calling.

I just want to live my life so, some day, I will get to see her again. But, for now, I want to serve the Lord and be myself.

Mama passed at 97 years old.

Little Girl Sucking Her Thumb

Little girl sucking her thumb
Looks at the little figurine,
But I can't see her through my tears.

The little girl sucking her thumb…
Mama left her thru all these years.

As I stop mourning for a while,
She always makes me smile,
And God will see me through.

Sometimes, life is dark and gloomy
Because my Mom is gone…

But sometimes I am happy
Just to know that I'm blessed to carry on.

Every day, it is hard to explain.
The sorrow never seems to end…

But I have not lost hope at all,
For Jesus is my friend.

Miss You

I wish I could text Mama in heaven
And tell her how I have missed her since she's been gone.

If I could walk down the streets of heaven,
I would bring her a thousand balloons.

A flower on her grave is about all that I can give.

If your mother has not gone on yet,
Give her flowers while she lives.

That goes for Daddies too.
We hold them in our hearts.

So, get right with your parents.
They play an important part.

Always give them honor, because, God,
I know He cares.

Give them love and devotion,
And the sincerity of your prayers.

www.ingramcontent.com/pod-product-compliance
Lightning Source LLC
Chambersburg PA
CBHW061730070526
44583CB00024B/3084